365 Days of Cats: Inspirational Quotes for the Cat Lover

Foreword by M.G. Keefe

365 Days of Cats:

Inspirational Quotes for the Cat Lover

Hot Tropica Books Publication

November 2012

Copyright © 2012 Foreword by M.G. Keefe

Cover illustration copyright © Jackson Falls

ISBN: Not assigned

Published by: **Hot Tropica Books**

365 Days of Cats

There is no creature more mysterious, and more fascinating than a cat. Cats fill our history books alongside their human owners and are often a subject of artwork.

This collection of memorable quotes is meant to inspire and amuse the cat lover in all of us. Start the day off with a smile by reading a cat quote every day of the year or just read the book in one sitting.

This book also makes a terrific gift for the cat lover.

To err is human, to purr is feline. ~ Robert Byrne

Foreword by MG Keefe

I love cats, and have always owned one or more for as long as I can remember. My first pet was a little black kitten that was sweet and cuddly when it was sleeping, and a bundle of pouncing furry energy when it was playing. I learned to pull a string along and the little kitten would pounce it on it and try to eat it as if the string was a mouse, but when the claws came out he was gentle around me. He was careful not to hurt me too badly or to dig his claws in too deeply. My scratches were well deserved and because of my age when I was playing too rough with him.

I am not the only one who has been fascinated with our feline fiends. Cats have been around humans for thousands of years. Sometimes we keep them in our home, and sometimes they are outdoor animals and roam free. Most of my friends who own a barn keep a barncat to keep their feed and barns mouse free and therefore snake free as well.

Cats are useful as well as loving pets.

You don't have to love cats to enjoy this book. The following collection of quotes are some of the funniest, most lovable, or more thoughtful quotes about cats in history.

Enjoy one a day to start your day off right or just read it through in one sitting. Either way, you are sure to enjoy it if you love cats.

365 Days of Cats

Day 1: No matter how much cats fight, there always seems to be plenty of kittens. ~ Abraham Lincoln

Day 2: I like pigs. Dogs look up to us. Cats look down upon us. Pigs treat us as equals. ~ Winston Churchill

Day 3: Don't think that I'm silly for liking it, I just happen to like the simple little things, and I like cats! ~ Michelle Gardner

Day 4: You can keep a dog; but it is the cat who keeps people, because cats find humans useful domestic animals. ~ George Mikes

Day 5: You own a dog but you feed a cat. ~ Jenny de Vries

Day 6: Thousands of years ago, cats were worshipped as gods. Cats have never forgotten this. ~ Anonymous

Day 7: A cat sees no good reason why it should obey another animal, even if it does stand on two legs. ~ Sarah Thompson

Day 8: One must love a cat on its own terms. ~ Paul Gray

Day 9: I have studied many philosophers and many cats. The wisdom of cats is infinitely superior. ~ Hippolyte Taine

Day 10: Cats never strike a pose which isn't photogenic. ~ Lillian Jackson Braun

Day 11: Dogs come when they're called; cats take a message and get back to you later. ~ Mary Bly

Day 12: If a dog jumps into your lap it is because he is fond of you; but if a cat does the same thing it is because your lap is warmer. ~ A. N. Whitehead

Day 13: I love cats because I enjoy my home; and little by little, they become its visible soul. ~ Jean Cocteau

Day 14: A meow massages the heart. ~ Stuart McMillan

Day 15: There are two means of refuge from the miseries of life: music and cats. ~ Albert Schweitzer

Day 16: There are no ordinary cats. ~ Colette

Day 17: With the qualities of cleanliness, affection, patience, dignity, and courage that cats have, how many of us, I ask you, would be capable of becoming cats? ~ Fernand Mery

Day 18: The smallest feline is a masterpiece. ~ Leonardo da Vinci

Day 19: Everything I know I learned from my cat: When you are hungry, eat. When you're tired nap in a sunbeam. When you go to the vets pee on your owner. ~ Gary Smith

Day 20: Of all God's creatures, there's only one that cannot be made slave of the lash. That one is the cat. If man could be crossed with the cat it would improve the man, but it would deteriorate the cat. ~ Mark Twain

Day 21: I have noticed that what cats most appreciate in a human being is not the ability to produce food which they take for granted--but his or her entertainment value. ~ Geoffrey Household

Day 22: Cats can be cooperative when something feels good, which, to a cat, is the way everything is supposed to feel as much of the time as possible. ~ Roger Caras

Day 23: Her function is to sit and be admired. ~ Georgina Strickland Gates

Day 24: Cats are intended to teach us that not everything in nature has a purpose. ~ Garrison Keillor

Day 25: By and large, people who enjoy teaching animals to roll over will find themselves happier with a dog. ~ Barbara Holland

Day 26: Meow is like aloha ~ it can mean anything. ~ Hank Ketchum

Day 27: If we treated everyone we meet with the same affection we bestow upon our favorite cat, they, too, would purr. ~ Martin Buxbaum

Day 28: Like a graceful vase, a cat, even when motionless, seems to flow. ~ George F. Will

Day 29: Cats seem to go on the principle that it never does any harm to ask for what you want. ~ Joseph Wood Krutch

Day 30: If you want to write, keep cats. ~ Aldous Huxley

Day 31: Cats always know whether people like or dislike them. They do not always care enough to do anything about it. ~ Winifred Carriere

Day 32: There's no need for a piece of sculpture in a home that has a cat. ~ Wesley Bates

Day 33: The phrase "domestic cat" is an oxymoron. ~ George F. Will

Day 34: A cat pours his body on the floor like water. It is restful just to see him. ~ William Lyon Phelps

Day 35: Prose book are the show dogs I breed and sell to support my cat. ~ Robert Graves

Day 36: As every cat owner knows, nobody owns a cat. ~ Ellen Perry Berkeley

Day 37: The really great thing about cats is their endless variety. One can pick a cat to fit almost any kind of decor, color, scheme, income, personality, mood. But under the fur, whatever color it may be, there still lies, essentially unchanged, one of the world's free souls. ~ Eric Gurney

Day 38: We have a theory that cats are planning to take over the world, just try to look them straight in the eye...yup, they're hiding something! ~ Dog Fancy

Day 39: The trouble with cats is that they've got no tact. ~ P. G. Wodehouse

Day 40: With their qualities of discretion, affection, patience, dignity, and courage, how many of us, I ask you would be capable of becoming cats? ~ Fernand Mery

Day 41: Cats' hearing apparatus is built to allow the human voice to easily go in one ear and out the other. ~ Stephen Baker

Day 42: If animals could speak the dog would be a a blundering outspoken fellow, but the cat would have the rare grace of never saying a word too much. ~ Mark Twain

Day 43: How we behave toward cats here below determines our status in heaven. ~ Robert A. Heinlein

Day 44: The mathematical probability of a common cat doing exactly as it pleases is the one scientific absolute in the world. ~ Lynn M. Osband

Day 45: Prowling his own quiet backyard or asleep by the fire, he is still only a whisker away from the wilds. ~ Jean Burden

Day 46: Cats do not have to be shown how to have a good time, for they are unfailing ingenious in that respect. ~ James Mason

Day 47: Even the stupidest cat seems to know more than any dog. ~ Eleanor Clark

Day 48: In the beginning, God created man, but seeing him so feeble, He gave him the cat. ~ Warren Eckstein

Day 49: We cannot without becoming cats, perfectly understand the cat mind. ~ St. George Mivart

Day 50: Cats are tigers of us poor devils. ~ Theophil Gautier

Day 51: Some people say that cats are sneaky, evil, and cruel. True, and they have many other fine qualities as well. ~ Missy Dizick

Day 52: As every cat owner knows, nobody owns a cat. ~ Ellen Perry Berkeley

Day 53: Most cats, when they are Out want to be In, and vice versa, and often simultaneously. ~ Louis F. Camuti, DVM

Day 54: I believe cats to be spirits come to earth. A cat, I am sure, could walk on a cloud without coming through. ~ Jules Verne

Day 55: You can't own a cat. The best you can do is be partners. ~ Sir Harry Swanson

Day 56: Most beds sleep up to six cats. Ten cats without the owner. ~ Stephen Baker

Day 57: By associating with the cat, one only risks becoming richer. ~ Colette

Day 58: I put down my book, The Meaning of Zen, and see the cat smiling into her fur as she delicately combs it with her rough pink tongue.
Cat, I would lend you this book to study but it appears you have already read it.
She looks up and gives me her full gaze.
Don't be ridiculous, she purrs, I wrote it.
~ from "Miao" by Dilys Laing

Day 59: The cat is domestic only as far as suits its own ends... ~ Saki (H. H. Munro)

Day 60: Purring is an automatic safety valve for dealing with happiness overflow. ~Anonymous

Day 61: Cats are smarter than dogs. You can't get eight cats to pull a sled through snow. ~ Jeff Valdez

Day 62: Intelligence in the cat is underrated. ~ Louis Wain

Day 63: Cats know how to obtain food without labor, shelter without confinement and love without penalties. ~ W. L. George

Day 64: Of all animals, the cat alone attains to the comtemplative life. He regards the wheel of existence from without, like the Buddha. ~ Andrew Lang

Day 65: There are few things in life more heartwarming than to be welcomed by a cat. ~ Tay Hohoff

Day 66: There is no more intrepid explorer than a kitten. ~ Jules Champfleury

Day 67: Even overweight, cats instinctively know the cardinal rule: when fat, arrange yourself in slim poses. ~ John Weitz

Day 68: Way down deep, we're all motivated by the same urges. Cats have the courage to live by them. ~ Jim Davis

Day 69: Two things are aesthetically perfect in the world ~ the clock and the cat. ~ Emile Auguste Chartier

Day 70: Confront a child, a puppy, and a kitten with sudden danger; the child will turn instinctively for assistance, the puppy will grovel in abject submission, the kitten will brace its tiny body for a frantic resistance. ~ Saki

Day 71: If a cat did not put a firm paw down now and then, how could his human remain possessed. ~ Winifred Carriere

Day 72: The cat seldom interferes with other people's rights. His intelligence keeps him from doing many of the fool things that complicate life. ~ Carl Van Vechten

Day 73: There are many intelligent species in the universe. They are all owned by cats. ~ Anonymous

Day 74: You cannot look at a sleeping cat and feel tense. ~ Jane Pauley

Day 75: There are two means of refuge from the miseries of life: music and cats. Albert Schweitzer

Day 76: Managing senior programmers is like herding cats. ~ Dave Platt

Day 77: Cats are rather delicate creatures and they are subject to a lot of ailments, but I never heard of one who suffered from insomnia. ~ Joseph Wood Crutch

Day 78: A cat sees us as the dogs...A cat sees himself as the human. ~ Unknown

Day 79: There is the little matter of disposal of droppings in which the cat is far ahead of its rivals. The dog is somehow thrilled by what he or any of his friends have produced, hates to leave it, adores smelling it, and sometimes eats it...The cat covers it up if he can... ~ Paul Gallico

Day 80: No tame animal has lost less of its native dignity or maintained more of its ancient reserve. The domestic cat may rebel tomorrow. ~ William Conway

Day 81: People who hate cats, will come back as mice in their next life. ~ Faith Resnick

Day 82: Cats are designated friends. ~ Norman Corwin

Day 83: There is no snooze button on a cat who wants breakfast. ~ Unknown

Day 84: Most cats, when they are out want to be in, and visa versa, and often simultaneously. ~ Louis J. Camuti

Day 85: The cat could very well be man's best friend but would never stoop to admitting it. ~ Doug Larson

Day 86: I found out why cats drink out of the toilet. My mother told me it's because the water is cold in there. And I'm like: How did my mother know that? ~ Wendy Liebman

Day 87: Cats are glorious creatures ~ who must on no accounts be underestimated... Their eyes are fathomless depths of cat-world mysteries. ~ Lesley Anne Ivory

Day 88: One of the oldest human needs is having someone to wonder where you are when you don't come home at night. ~ Margaret Mead

Day 89: One is never sure, watching two cats washing each other, whether it's affection, the taste or a trial run for the jugular. ~ Helen Thomson

Day 90: Animals are such agreeable friends — they ask no questions, they pass no judgment. ~ George Eliot

Day 91: One reason we admire cats is for their proficiency in one-upmanship. They always seem to come out on top, no matter what they are doing, or pretend they do. ~ Barbara Webster

Day 92: As anyone who has ever been around a cat for any length of time well knows, cats have enormous patience with the limitations of the human mind. ~ Cleveland Amory

Day 93: Cats are a tonic, they are a laugh, they are a cuddle, they are at least pretty just about all of the time and beautiful some of the time. ~ Roger Caras

Day 94: When I play with my cat, who knows if I am not a pastime to her more than she is to me? ~ Montaigne

Day 95: Cats are a mysterious kind of folk. There is more passing in their minds than we are aware of. ~ Sir Walter Scott

Day 96: If you are worthy of its affection, a cat will be your friend, but never your slave. ~ Theophile Gautier

Day 97: Of all animals, he alone attains to the Contemplative Life. ~ Andrew Lang

Day 98: Cats are kindly masters, just so long as you remember your place. ~ Paul Gray

Day 99: Some people say that cats are sneaky, evil, and cruel. True, and they have many other fine qualities as well. ~ Missy Dizick

Day 100: One of the ways in which cats show happiness is by sleeping. ~ Cleveland Amory

Day 101: Cats are intended to teach us that not everything in nature has a function. ~ Garrison Keillor

Day 102: There are many intelligent species in the universe. They are all owned by cats. ~ Unknown

Day 103: Cats do care. For example they know instinctively what time we have to be at work in the morning and they wake us up twenty minutes before the alarm goes off.~ Michael Nelson

Day 104: When you are looking, a cat acts like a princess, but the minute they think you are not looking, a cat acts like a fool. ~ KC Buffington

Day 105: The smart cat doesn't let on that he is. ~ H.G. Frommer

Day 106: His mind is like a steel trap--full of mice. ~ Foghorn Leghorn

Day 107: Cats seem to go on the principle that it never does any harm to ask for what you want.~ Joseph Wood Crutch

Day 108: It always gives me a shiver when I see a cat seeing what I can't see. ~ Eleanor Farjeon

Day 109: People that hate cats will come back as mice in their next life. ~ Faith Resnick

Day 110: A baited cat may grow fierce as a lion. ~ Samuel Palmer

Day 111: If man could be crossed with the cat it would improve man, but it would deteriorate the cat. ~ Mark Twain

Day 112: Cats are notoriously sore losers. Coming in second best, especially to someone as poorly coordinated as a human being, grates their sensibility. ~ Stephen Baker

Day 113: Winners are different. They're a different breed of cat. ~ Byron Nelson

Day 114: Of all domestic animals the cat is the most expressive. His face is capable of showing a wide range of expressions. His tail is a mirror of his mind. His gracefulness is surpassed only by his agility. And, along with all these, he has a sense of humor. ~ Walter Chandoha

Day 115: One of the most striking differences between a cat and a lie is that a cat only has nine lives. ~ Mark Twain

Day 116: He [the cat] liked to peep into the refrigerator and risk having his head shut in by the closing door. He also climbed to the top of the stove, discontinuing the practice after he singed his tail. ~ Lloyd Alexander

Day 117: An ordinary kitten will ask more questions than any five year old. ~ Carl Van Vechten

Day 118: Essentially, you do not so much teach your cat as bribe him. ~ Lynn Hollyn

Day 119: You may own a cat, but cannot govern one. ~ Kate Sanborn

Day 120: Women, poets, and especially artists like cats; delicate natures only can realize their sensitive systems. ~ Helen M. Winslow

Day 121: If you yell at a cat, you're the one who is making a fool of yourself. ~ Unknown

Day 122: Time spent with cats is never wasted. ~ May Sarton

Day 123: The reason cats climb is so that they can look down on almost every other animal...its also the reason they hate birds. ~ KC Buffington

Day 124: Way down deep we are all motivated by the same urges, cats have the courage to live by them. ~ Jim Davis

Day 125: If God created man in his own image, you've got to wonder; in whose image did he create the nobler cat? ~ Unknown

Day 126: Cats can work out mathematically the exact place to sit that will cause most inconvenience. ~ Pam Brown

Day 127: Two cats can live as cheaply as one, and their owner has twice as much fun. ~ Lloyd Alexander

Day 128: A dog is like a liberal, he wants to please everybody. A cat doesn't really need to know that everybody loves him. ~ William Kunstler

Day 129: There are few things in life more heart warming than to be welcomed by a cat. ~ Tay Hohoff

Day 130: Cats posses so many of the same qualities as some people that it is often hard to tell the people and the cats apart. ~ P.J. O'Rourke

Day 131: It is remarkable, in cats, that the outer life they reveal to their masters is one of perpetual boredom. ~ Robley Wilson, Jr.

Day 132: If the pull of the outside world is strong, there is also a pull towards the human. The cat may disappear on its own errands, but sooner or later, it returns once again for a little while, to greet us with its own type of love. Independent as they are, cats find more than pleasure in our company. ~ Lloyd Alexander

Day 133: There is no cat 'language'. Painful as it is for us to admit, they don't need one. ~ Barbara Holland

Day 134: Cat said, 'I am not a friend, and I am not a Servant. I am the Cat who walks by himself, and I wish to come into your Cave. ~ Rudyard Kipling, from the 'Just-So Stories'

Day 135: The furry little buggers [cats] are just deep, deep wells you throw your emotions into. ~ Bruce Schimmel

Day 136: Cats were put into the world to disprove the dogma that all things were created to serve man. ~ Paul Gray

Day 137: Cats have an infallible understanding of total concentration--and get between you and it. ~ Arthur Bridges

Day 138: To err is human, to purr is feline. ~ Robert Byrne

Day 139: A kitten is so flexible that she is almost double; the hind parts are equivalent to another kitten with which the forepart plays. She does not discover that her tail belongs to her until you tread on it. ~ Henry David Thoreau

Day 140: Ignorant people think it is the noise which fighting cats make that is so aggravating, but it ain't so; it is the sickening grammar they use. ~ Mark Twain

Day 141: If you want to know the character of a man, find out what his cat thinks of him. ~ Anonymous

Day 142: Dogs eat. Cats dine. ~ Ann Taylor

Day 143: The smallest feline is a masterpiece. ~ Leonardo Da Vinci

Day 144: You are my cat and I am your human. ~ Hilaire Belloc

Day 145: Our perfect companions never have fewer than four feet. ~ Colette

Day 146: I've met many thinkers and many cats, but the wisdom of cats is infinitely superior. ~ Hippolyte Taine

Day 147: The ideal of calm exists in a sitting cat. ~ Jules Reynard

Day 148: A cat is there when you call her ~ if she doesn't have something better to do. ~ Bill Adler

Day 149: If cats could talk, they wouldn't. ~ Nan Porter

Day 150: The only mystery about the cat is why it ever decided to become a domestic animal. ~ Sir Compton MacKenzie

Day 151: Every life should have nine cats. ~ Anonymous

Day 152: Since each of us is blessed with only one life, why not live it with a cat? ~ Robert Stearns

Day 153: The little furry buggers are just deep, deep wells you throw all your emotions into. ~ Bruce Schimmel

Day 154: A cat can purr its way out of anything. ~ Donna McCrohan

Day 155: A meow massages the heart. ~ Stuart McMillan

Day 156: My cat does not talk as respectfully to me as I do to her. ~ Colette

Day 157: A cat is a puzzle for which there is no solution. ~ Hazel Nicholson

Day 158: It is in their eyes that their magic resides. ~ Arthur Symons

Day 159: Meow is like aloha ~ it can mean anything. ~ Hank Ketchum

Day 160: Cats, no less liquid than a shadow, offer no angles to the wind. They slip, diminished, neat, through loopholes less than themselves. ~ A.S.J. Tessimond

Day 161: Dogs come when they're called; cats take a message and get back to you. ~ Mary Bly

Day 162: A dog is a dog, a bird is a bird, and a cat is a person. ~ Mugsy Peabody

Day 163: I think one reason we admire cats, those of us who do, is their proficience in one-upmanship. They always seem to come out on top, no matter what they are doing--or pretend to do. Rarely do you see a cat discomfited. They have no conscience, and they never regret. Maybe we secretly envy them. ~ Barbara Webster, from "Creatures and Contentments"

Day 164: Some cats is blind, And stone-deaf some, But ain't no cat Wuz ever dumb. ~ Anthony Euwer

Day 165: Most cats, when they are Out want to be In, and vice versa, and often simultaneously. ~ Dr. Louis J. Camuti

Day 166: The cat has been described as the most perfect animal, the acme of muscular perfection and the supreme example in the animal kingdom of the coordination of mind and muscle. ~ Roseanne Ambrose Brown

Day 167: If your cat falls out of a tree, go indoors to laugh. ~ Patricia Hitchcock

Day 168: Poets generally love cats--because poets have no delusions about their own superiority. ~ Marion Garretty

Day 169: Any cat who misses a mouse pretends it was aiming for the dead leaf. ~ Charlotte Gray

Day 170: There is nothing in the animal world, to my mind, more delightful than grown cats at play. They are so swift and light and graceful, so subtle and designing, and yet so richly comical. ~ Monica Edwards

Day 171: Everything a cat is and does physically is to me beautiful, lovely, stimulating, soothing, attractive and an enchantment. ~ Paul Gallico, from "An Honourable Cat"

Day 172: French novelist Colette was a firm cat-lover. When she was in the U.S. she saw a cat sitting in the street. She went over to talk to it and the two of them mewed at each other for a friendly minute. Colette turned to her companion and exclaimed, "Enfin! Quelqu'un qui parle francais." (At last! Someone who speaks French!) ~ Anonymous

Day 173: A cat isn't fussy--just so long as you remember he likes his milk in the shallow, rose-patterned saucer and his fish on the blue plate. From which he will take it, and eat it off the floor. ~ Arthur Bridges

Day 174: It is a very inconvenient habit of kittens (Alice had once made the remark) that whatever you say to them, they /always/ purr. ~ Lewis Carroll

Day 175: A cat can maintain a position of curled up somnolence on your knee until you are nearly upright. To the last minute she hopes your conscience will get the better of you and you will settle down again. ~ Pam Brown

Day 176: One small cat changes coming home to an empty house to coming home. ~ Pam Brown

Day 177: A cat allows you to sleep on the bed. On the edge. ~ Jenny de Vries

Day 178: To some blind souls all cats are much alike. To a cat lover every cat from the beginning of time has been utterly and amazingly unique. ~ Jenny de Vries

Day 179: All cats like being the focus of attention. ~ Peter Gray

Day 180: For every house is incomplete without him, and a blessing is lacking in spirit. ~ Christopher Smart

Day 181: The trouble with sharing one's bed with cats is that they'd rather sleep on you than beside you. ~ Pam Brown

Day 182: There are people who reshape the world by force or argument, but the cat just lies there, dozing, and the world quietly reshapes itself to suit his comfort and convenience. ~ Allen and Ivy Dodd

Day 183: Many a cat can only be lured in by switching off all the lights and keeping very still. Until the indignant cry of a cat-locked-out comes at the door. ~ Pam Brown

Day 184: Places to look: behind the books in the bookshelf, any cupboard with a gap too small for any cat to squeeze through, the top of anything sheer, under anything too low for a cat to squash under and inside the piano. ~ Roseanne Ambrose-Brown

Day 185: Cats like doors left open--in case they change their minds. ~ Rosemary Nisbet

Day 186: When I play with my cat, who knows if I am not a pastime to her more than she is to me? ~ Michel E. de Monaigne

Day 187: Nobody who is not prepared to spoil cats will get from them the reward they are able to give to those who do spoil them. ~ Compton MacKenzie

Day 188: If you shamefully misuse a cat once she will always maintain a dignified reserve toward you afterward. You will never get her full confidence again. ~ Mark Twain

Day 189: People meeting for the first time suddenly relax if they find they both have cats. And plunge into anecdote. ~ Charlotte Gray

Day 190: The purity of a man's heart can be quickly measure by how they regard cats. ~ Anonymous

Day 191: It's very hard to be polite if you're a cat. ~ Anonymous

Day 192: It is in the nature of cats to do a certain amount of unescorted roaming. ~ Adlai Stevenson

Day 193: Women and cats will do as they please, and men and dogs should relax and get used to the idea. ~ Robert A. Heinlein

Day 194: Most cats do not approach humans recklessly. The possibility of concealed weapons, clods or sticks, tend to make them reserved. Homeless cats in particular--with some justification, unfortunately--consider humans their natural enemies. Much ceremony must be observed, and a number of diplomatic feelers put out, before establishing a state of truce. ~ Lloyd Alexander

Day 195: When addressed, a gentleman cat does not move a muscle. He looks as if he hasn't heard. ~ Mary Sarton

Day 196: The cat of the slums and alleys, starved, outcast, harried, ... still displays the self-reliant watchfulness which man has never taught it to lay aside. ~ Saki

Day 197: Again I must remind you that a dog's a dog--a cat's a cat. ~ T. S. Eliot

Day 198: When I play with my cat, who knows if I am not a pastime to her more than she to me? ~ Montaigne

Day 199: Who can believe that there is no soul behind those luminous eyes! ~ Theophile Gautier

Day 200: God made the cat that man might have the pleasure of caressing the lion. ~ Fernand Mery

Day 201: When anyone mistreats it, the cat wants nothing more to do with that person and will remember him or her for a long time. It doesn't believe in the doctrine of turning the other cheek and won't pretend that it does. ~ Lawrence N. Johnson

Day 202: I purr, therefore I am. ~ Anonymous

Day 203: A cat is the only domestic animal I know who toilet trains itself and does a damned impressive job of it. ~ Joseph Epstein

Day 204: People that don't like cats haven't met the right one yet. ~ Deborah A. Edwards, D.V.M.

Day 205: Your cat may never have to hunt farther than the kitchen counter for its supper nor face a predator more fierce than the vacuum cleaner... ~ Barbara L. Diamond

Day 206: I saw the most beautiful cat today. It was sitting by the side of the road, its two front feet neatly and graciously together. Then it gravely swished around its tail to completely encircle itself. It was so fit and beautifully neat, that gesture, and so self-satisfied, so complacent. ~ Ann Morrow Lindbergher

Day 207: Cats are living adornments. ~ Edwin Lent

Day 208: What greater gift than the love of a cat? ~ Charles Dickens

Day 209: The cat is above all things, a dramatist. ~ Margaret Benson

Day 210: A kitten is the delight of the household; all day long a comedy is played out by an incomparable actor. ~ Champfleury

Day 211: A cat doesn't know what it wants and wants more of it. ~ Richard Hexem

Day 212: Even if you have just destroyed a Ming Vase, purr. Usually all will be forgiven. ~ Lenny Rubenstein

Day 213: Just as the would-be debutante will fret and fuss over every detail till all is perfect, so will the fastidious feline patiently toil until every whiskertip is in place. ~ Lynn Hollyn

Day 214: Does the father figure in your cat's life ever clean the litter box? My husband claims that men lack the scooping gene. ~ Barbara L. Diamond

Day 215: Another cat? Perhaps. For love there is also a season; its seeds must be resown. But a family cat is not replaceable like a wornout coat or a set of tires. Each new kitten becomes its own cat, and none is repeated. I am four cats old, measuring out my life in friends that have succeeded but not replaced one another. ~ Irving Townsend

Day 216: My cat speaks sign language with her tail. ~ Robert A. Stern

Day 217: A home without a cat, and a well-fed, well-petted and properly revered cat, may be a perfect home, perhaps; but how can it prove its title? ~ Mark Twain

Day 218: If by chance I seated myself to write, she very slyly, very tenderly, seeking protection and caresses, would softly take her place on my knee and follow the comings and goings of my pen -~ sometimes effacing, with an unintentional stroke of her paw, lines of whose tenor she disapproved. ~ Pierre Loti

Day 219: A cat is nobody's fool. ~ Heywood Brown

Day 220: Cat: A pygmy lion who loves mice, hates dogs, and patronizes human beings. ~ Oliver Herford

Day 221: Some people say that cats are sneaky, evil, and cruel. True, and they have many other fine qualities as well. ~ Missy Dizick

Day 222: A cat's got her own opinion of human beings. She don't say much, but you can tell enough to make you anxious not to hear the whole of it. ~ Jerome K. Jerome

Day 223: If stretching were wealth, the cat would be rich. ~ Unknown

Day 224: I would gladly change places with any of my cats. ~ George Ney

Day 225: It's really the cat's house--we just pay the mortgage. ~ Unknown

Day 226: The key to a successful new relationship between a cat and human is patience. ~ Susan Easterly

Day 227: Most cats are not shy about letting their people know what they want. ~ Karen Duprey

Day 228: A cat's name may tell you more about its owners than it does about the cat. ~ Linda W. Lewis

Day 229: Four little Persians, but only one looked in my direction. I extended a tentative finger and two soft paws clung to it. There was a contented sound of purring, I suspect on both our parts. ~ George Freedley

Day 230: The cat has too much spirit to have no heart. ~ Ernest Menault

Day 231: Who needs television when you have cats? ~ Lori Spigelmyer

Day 232: Some people own cats and go on to lead normal lives. ~ Unknown

Day 233: You never saw such a crazy cat. 'Up the wall' took on a literal meaning. ~ Arnold Hano

Day 234: I called my cat William because no shorter name fits the dignity of his character. Poor old man, he has fits now, so I call him Fitz-William. ~ Josh Billings

Day 235: It was not I who was teaching my cat to gather rosebuds, but she who was teaching me. ~ Irving Townsend

Day 236: Always the cat remains a little beyond the limits we try to set for him in our blind folly. ~ Andre Norton

Day 237: If there was any petting to be done...he chose to do it. Often he would sit looking at me, and then, moved by a delicate affection, come and pull at my coat and sleeve until he could touch my face with his nose, and then go away contented. ~ Charles Dudley Warner

Day 238: People who love cats have some of the biggest hearts around. ~ Susan Easterly

Day 239: For me, one of the pleasures of cats' company is their devotion to bodily comfort. ~ Sir Compton Mackenzie

Day 240: When all candles be out, all cats be gray. ~ John Heywood

Day 241: The cat does not offer services. The cat offers itself. Of course he wants care and shelter. You don't buy love for nothing. Like all pure creatures, cats are practical. ~ William S. Burroughs

Day 242: Is it yet another survival of jungle instinct, this hiding away from prying eyes at important times? Or merely a gesture of independence, a challenge to man and his stupid ways? ~ Michael Joseph

Day 243: Although all cat games have their rules and rituals, these vary with the individual player. The cat, of course, never breaks a rule. If it does not follow precedent, that simply means it has created a new rule and it is up to you to learn it quickly if you want the game to continue. ~ Sidney Denham

Day 244: When your cat rubs the side of its face along your leg, it's affectionately marking you with its scent, identifying you as its private property, saying, in effect, 'You belong to me'. ~ Susan McDonough, D.M.V.

Day 245: Cats do care. For example, they know instinctively what time we have to be at work in the morning; and they wake us up twenty minutes before the alarm goes off. ~ Michael Nelson

Day 246: A cat is never vulgar. ~ Carl Van Vechten

Day 247: Cats are dangerous companions for writers because cat watching is a near-perfect method of writing avoidance. ~ Dan Greenburg

Day 248: I rarely meddled in the cat's personal affairs and she rarely meddled in mine. Neither of us was foolish enough to attribute human emotions to our pets. ~ Kinky Friedman

Day 249: Cats are successful underachievers. They only need to purr in order to get free food and TLC. What other creature can lay around the house doing nothing beyond purring, and still get free food and TLC? ~ Jim Aites

Day 250: To respect the cat is the beginning of the aesthetic sense. ~ Erasmus Darwin

Day 251: Cat people are different to the extent that they generally are not conformists. How could they be with a cat running their lives? ~ Louis J. Camuti, D.V.M.

Day 252: Sleeping together is a euphemism for people, but tantamount to marriage with cats. ~ Marge Percy

Day 253: Could the purr be anything but contemplative? ~ Irving Townsend

Day 254: Cats are much like they were when they were first domesticated. They are very independent because they had to be to survive. ~ Dr. Raymond Hampton

Day 255: Any conditioned cat-hater can be won over by any cat who chooses to make the effort. ~ Paul Corey

Day 256: You can tell your cat anything and he'll still love you. If you lose your job or your best friend, your cat will think no less of you. ~ Helen Powers

Day 257: Cats are connoisseurs of comfort. ~ James Herriot

Day 258: A cat can be trusted to purr when she is pleased, which is more than can be said for human beings. ~ William Ralph Inge

Day 259: Cats come and go without ever leaving. ~ Martha Curtis

Day 260: Those who play with cats must expect to get scratched. ~ Cervantes

Day 261: Actually cats do this to protect you from gnomes who come and steal your breath while your sleep. ~ John Dobbin

Day 262: Are cats lazy? Well, more power to them if they are. Which one of us has not entertained the dream of doing just as he likes, when and how he likes, and as much as he likes? ~ Fernand Mery

Day 263: He seems the incarnation of everything soft and silky and velvety, without a sharp edge in his composition, a dreamer whose philosophy is sleep and let sleep. ~ Saki

Day 264: The way to keep a cat is to try to chase it away. ~ E. W. Howe

Day 265: If I called her she would pretend not to hear, but would come a few moments later when it could appear that she had thought of doing so first. ~ Arthur Weigall

Day 266: A little drowsing cat is an image of perfect beatitude. ~ Jules Champfleury

Day 267: A cat sleeps fat, yet walks thin. ~ Unknown

Day 268: All cats are possessed of a proud spirit, and the surest way to forfeit the esteem of a cat is to treat him as an inferior being. ~ Michael Joseph

Day 269: There is no such thing as 'just a cat'. ~ Robert A. Heinlein

Day 270: Cats, like men, are flatterers. ~ Waltor Savage Landor

Day 271: Every cat is special in its own way. ~ Sara Jane Clark

Day 272: There is, indeed, no single quality of the cat that man could not emulate to his advantage. ~ Carl Van Vechten

Day 273: We should be careful to get out of an experience only the wisdom that is in it and stop there, lest we be like the cat that sits down on a hot stove-lid. She will never sit down on a hot stove-lid again, and that is well; but also she will never sit down on a cold one anymore. ~ Mark Twain

Day 274: Artists like cats; soldiers like dogs. ~ Desmond Morris

Day 275: The reason cats climb is so that they can look down on almost every other animal...it's also the reason they hate birds. ~ K.C. Buffington

Day 276: When I raise a cat from kittenhood, it learns to read me so well that it can con me and predict what I'm going to do. A young adult cat doesn't know what to expect from me and I don't know what to expect from it, so we immediately have each other's attention. ~ Karl Lewis Miller

Day 277: A kitten is chiefly remarkable for rushing about like mad at nothing whatever, and generally stopping before it gets there. ~ Agnes Repplier

Day 278: The whir of a can opener or the bark of an unfamiliar dog...will send even the most deeply dozing cat bounding into the kitchen or under the bed. ~ Barbara L. Diamond

Day 279: Cats are smart. You know it and I know it. ~ Debbie Mertens

Day 280: Beware of those who dislike cats. ~ Unknown

Day 281: If you would know what a cat is thinking about, you must hold its paw in your hand for a long time. ~ Jules Champfleury

Day 282: Many cats simply pounce to their own drummers. ~ Karen Duprey

Day 283: I am indebted to the species of the cat for a particular kind of honorable deceit, for a great control over myself, for characteristic aversion to brutal sounds, and for the need to keep silent for long periods of time. ~ Colette

Day 284: Cats, like butterflies, need no excuse. ~ Robert A. Heinlein

Day 285: The domestic cat seems to have greater confidence in itself than in anyone else. ~ Lawrence N. Johnson

Day 286: Theology is never any help; it is searching in a dark cellar at midnight for a black cat that isn't there. Theologians can persuade themselves of anything. ~ Robert A. Heinlein

Day 287: Any household with at least one feline member has no need for an alarm clock. ~ Louise A. Belcher

Day 288: Cats conspire to keep us at arm's length. ~ Frank Perkins

Day 289: The way to get on with a cat is to treat it as an equal ~ or even better, as the superior it knows itself to be. ~ Elizabeth Peters

Day 290: People who own Siamese cats must make up their minds to do a good deal of waiting upon them. ~ Compton MacKenzie

Day 291: When Mother Nature saw fit to remove the tail of the Manx, she left, in place of the tail, more cat. ~ Mary E. Stewart

Day 292: He lives in the halflights in secret places, free and alone ~ this mysterious little great being whom his mistress calls 'My cat.' ~ Margaret Benson

Day 293: Cats look beyond appearances--beyond species entirely, it seems--to peer into the heart. ~ Barbara L. Diamond

Day 294: One cat just leads to another. ~ Ernest Hemingway

Day 295: A cat doesn't 'roll' well with a change of someone else's making. ~ Carole Wilbourn

Day 296: The cat is the only animal which accepts the comforts but rejects the bondage of domesticity. ~ Georges Louis Leclerc de Buffon

Day 297: I cannot deny that a cat lover and his cat have a master/slave relationship. The cat is the master. ~ Arthur R. Kassin

Day 298: A cat's behavior is a direct reflection of his feelings. ~ Carole Wilbourn

Day 299: My husband said it was him or the cat...I miss him sometimes. ~ Unknown

Day 300: Cats don't like change without their consent. ~ Roger A. Caras

Day 301: There are two means of refuge from the miseries of life: music and cats. ~ Albert Schweitzer

Day 302: Kittens believe that all nature is occupied with their diversion. ~ F.A. Paradis de Moncrif

Day 303: Cats have enormous patience with the limitations of the human mind. They realize...that we have an infuriating inability to understand, let alone follow, even the simplest and most explicit of directions. ~ Cleveland Amory

Day 304: Cats have intercepted my footsteps at the ankle for so long that my gait, both at home and on tour, has been compared to that of a man wading through low surf. ~ Roy Blount, Jr.

Day 305: To understand a cat, you must realize that he has his own gifts, his own viewpoint, even his own morality. ~ Lilian Jackson Braun

Day 306: In my next life, I'd like to come back as a cat. ~ Patti J. Moran

Day 307: It isn't always easy being a father to a cat. ~ B. L. Diamond

Day 308: A cat with kittens nearly always decides sooner or later to move them. ~ Sidney Denham

Day 309: A cat will do what it wants when it wants, and there's not a thing you can do about it. ~ Frank Perkins

Day 310: But nature does not say that cats are more valuable than mice; nature makes no remark on the subject. She does not even say the cat is enviable or the mouse pitiable. We think the cat superior because we have (or most of us have) a particular philosophy to the effect that life is better than death. But if the mouse were a German pessimist mouse, he might not think the cat had beaten him at all. He might have think he had beaten the cat by getting to the grave first. ~ Gilbert Keith Chesterton

Day 311: If a dog jumps into your lap, it is because he is fond of you; but if a cat does the same thing, it is because your lap is warmer. ~ Alfred North Whitehead

Day 312: If the claws didn't retract, cats would be like Velcro. ~ Dr. Bruce Fogle

Day 313: You have learned enough to see that cats are much like you and me. ~ T.S. Eliot

Day 314: The purr from cat to man says, 'You bring me happiness; I am at peace with you.' ~ Barbara L. Diamond

Day 315: The cat is mighty dignified until the dog comes by. ~ Unknown

Day 316: It doesn't do to be sentimental about cats; the best ones don't respect you for it. ~ Susan Howatch

Day 317: The cat, which is a solitary beast, is single minded and goes its way alone; but the dog, like his master, is confused in his mind. ~ H.G. Wells

Day 318: The man who carries a cat by the tail learns something that can be learned in no other way. ~ Mark Twain

Day 319: More than likely it was the cat who first coined and put into practice the sage advice: 'If you would have a thing done well, you must do it yourself.' ~ Lawrence N. Johnson

Day 320: The trouble with a kitten is that eventually it becomes a CAT. ~ Ogden Nash

Day 321: In reality, cats are probably better off remaining indoors and sending out their humans to deal with the outside world. ~ Dr. Phyllis Sherman Raschke

Day 322: He has become a much better cat than I have a person. With his gentle urgings, he made me realize that life doesn't end just because one has a few obstacles to overcome. ~ Mary F. Graf

Day 323: Bless their little pointed faces and their big, loyal, loving hearts. If a cat did not put a firm paw down now and then, how could his human remain possessed? ~ Winifred Carriere

Day 324: Some animals are secretive; some are shy. A cat is private. ~ Leonard Michaels

Day 325: Among animals, cats are the top-hatted, frock-coated statesmen going about their affairs at their own pace. ~ Robert Sterns

Day 326: Cats are creatures that express a multitude of moods and attitudes. ~ Karen Brademeyer

Day 327: Cats often devise their own sets of rules that they think we should live by, and they may be quick to chastise us if we fail to adhere to these rules! ~ Margaret Reister, D.V.M.

Day 328: Civilization is defined by the presence of cats. ~ Unknown

Day 329: The problem with cats is that they get the same exact look whether they see a moth or an axe murderer. ~ Paula Poundstone

Day 330: Curiosity killed the cat but for a while I was a suspect. ~ Steven Wright

Day 331: If I die before my cat, I want a little of my ashes put in his food so I can live inside him. ~ Drew Barrymore

Day 332: If a dog jumps in your lap, it is because he is fond of you; but if a cat does the same thing, it is because your lap is warmer. ~ Alfred North Whitehead

Day 333: The cat has too much spirit to have no heart. ~ Ernest Menaul

Day 334: Who can believe that there is no soul behind those luminous eyes! ~ Theophile Gautier

Day 335: If a cat does something, we call it instinct; if we do the same thing, for the same reason, we call it intelligence. ~ Will Cuppy

Day 336: If there is one spot of sunlight spilling onto the floor, a cat will find it and soak it up. ~ Joan Asper McIntosh

Day 337: As anyone who has ever been around a cat for any length of time well knows cats have enormous patience with the limitations of the human kind. ~ Cleveland Amory

Day 338: The ideal of calm exists in a sitting cat. ~ Jules Reynard

Day 339: A cat has absolute emotional honesty: human beings, for one reason or another, may hide their feelings, but a cat does not. ~ Ernest Hemingway

Day 340: Curiosity is the very basis of education and if you tell me curiosity killed the cat, I only say the cat died nobly. ~ Arnold Edinbrough

Day 341: Kittens are born with their eyes shut. They open them in about six days, take a look around, then close them again for the better part of their lives. ~ Stephen Baker

Day 342: No amount of time can erase the memory of a good cat, and no amount of masking tape can ever totally remove his fur from your couch. ~ Leo Dworken

Day 343: Cats are the ultimate narcissists. You can tell this by all the time they spend on personal grooming. Dogs aren't like this. A dog's idea of personal grooming is to roll in a dead fish. ~ James Gorman

Day 344: There is, incidently, no way of talking about cats that enables one to come off as a sane person. ~ Dan Greenberg

Day 345: "You can't help that. We're all mad here." ~ The Cheshire Cat from Alice in Wonderland

Day 346: Most cats when they are out, want to be in, and vice versa, and often simultaneously. ~ Dr. Louis J. Camuti

Day 347: Cats know how to obtain food without labor, shelter without confinement, and love without penalties. ~ Walter Lionel George

Day 348: The cat is the only animal without visible means of support who still manages to earn a living in the city. ~ Carl Van Vechten

Day 349: I must have a cat whom I find homeless, wandering about the court, and to whom, therefore, I am under no obligation. I have already selected a dirty little drunken wretch of a kitten to be the successor to my poor old cat. ~ Samuel Butler

Day 350: The artist is uncomfortable with his success and with the blizzard of fan mail it has produced. Kliban's recent collections have been conspicuously empty of cats. "Cats are wonderful," Kliban once said. "It's drawings of cats I get tired of." J.C. Suares in Great Cats

Day 351: I want to create cats I see crossing the streets, not like those you see in houses. They have nothing in common. The cat of the streets has bristling fur. It runs like a fiend, and if it looks at you, you think it is going to jump in your face. ~ Pablo Picasso.

Day 352: Cats can be very funny and have the oddest way of showing they are glad to see you. Rudimac always peed in our shoes. ~ W.H. Auden

Day 353: Recently we were discussing the possibility of making one of our cats Pope, and we decided the fact she was not Italian, and was female, made the third point, that she was a cat irrelevant. ~ Katharine Whitehorn

Day 354: A cat can climb down from a tree without the assistance of the fire department or any other agency. The proof is that no one has ever seen a cat skeleton in a tree. ~ Anonymous

Day 355: The human race may be divided into people who love cats and people who hate them; the neutrals being few in numbers, and for intellectual and moral reasons, not worth describing. ~ Agnes Repplier

Day 356: People with insufficient personalities are fond of cats. These people adore being ignored. ~ Henry Morgan

Day 357: Perhaps a child like a cat, is so much inside of himself that he does not see himself in the mirror. ~ Anais Nin

Day 358: Cats are oppressed, dogs terrify them, landladies starve them, boys stone them, everybody speaks of them with contempt. If they were human beings we could talk of their oppressors with a studied violence, add our strength to theirs, even organize the oppressed like good politicians sell our charity for power. ~ William Butler Yeats

Day 359: What's virtue in a man can't be virtue in a cat. ~ Gail Hamilton

Day 360: The ideal of calm exists in a sitting cat. ~ Jules Renard

Day 361:Nothing is so difficult as to paint a cat's face, which as Moncrif justly observes bears a character of 'finesse and hilarity'. The lines are so delicate, the eyes so strange, the movements subject to such sudden impulses, that one should be feline oneself to portray such a subject. ~ Champfleury (Jules Husson)

Day 362: I have seen how the cat trembles while sleeping. The night runs over him like dark water. ~ Pablo Neruda

Day 363: The behavior of men to animals and their behavior to each other bear a constant relationship. ~ Herbert Spencer

Day 364: Every contented cat is an "it". ~ Helen Powers on the Virtue of Neutering

Day 365: My cat has no name. We simply call him cat. He doesn't seem to blame anyone for that. For he

is not like us, who often, I'm afraid kick up quite a
fuss if our names are mislaid. ~ Vernon Scannell

8097812R00032

Printed in Great Britain
by Amazon.co.uk, Ltd.,
Marston Gate.